GREAT OPERA

ARIAS AND THEMES
FOR SOLO PIANO

50 Arrangements

CAROLINDA CARLSON

DOVER PUBLICATIONS, INC.
MINEOLA, NEW YORK

To the Pianist

A young musician will have a more complete education if he or she gains some knowledge of opera. Much of our beloved and beautiful music is to be found there. Opera dates back almost 400 years. The forty-three operas presented here comprise about half of the current repertoire, and represent nearly all major composers. If opera performances are not available in your area, you can still find the joy of opera music in these piano reductions. But plan for the future day when you can attend a live performance.

—C. C.

Copyright
Copyright © 2011, 2014 by Carolinda Carlson
All rights reserved.

Bibliographical Note
Great Opera Arias and Themes for Solo Piano: 50 Arrangements, first published by Dover Publications, Inc., in 2014, is a revised edition of *Grand Opera for Piano Students,* originally published by Carolinda Carlson in 2011.

International Standard Book Number
ISBN-13: 978-0-486-49280-3
ISBN-10: 0-486-49280-X

Manufactured in the United States by Courier Corporation
49280X01   2014
www.doverpublications.com

Contents

GREAT OPERA

ARIAS AND THEMES
FOR SOLO PIANO

50 Arrangements

THE ABDUCTION FROM THE SERAGLIO

Die Entführung aus dem Serail

se-rä´-(g)-li-o

German
Three acts.
Premiered in Vienna, Austria, 1782.
Libretto by G. Stephanie, from C. F. Bretzner, from J. Andre.

Set in the sixteenth century at a country estate. Constanza, a noblewoman, and her maid, have been captured by pirates and are enslaved at the palace of a powerful Turkish Pasha. The harem-keeper, Osmin, tries to pursue the maid, while the Pasha wants Constanza. Belmonte, a Spanish nobleman, is betrothed to Constanza. He plans an escape for the girls, but all are caught. Although the Pasha has a score to settle with Belmonte's family, he graciously releases the prisoners.

Wolfgang Amadeus Mozart
(1756–1791)

What Joy, What Delight
Welche wonne, welche lust

Act II. When the maid hears of the escape plan, she sings for joy.

AÏDA
ä-e´-da

Italian
Four acts.
Premiered in Cairo, Egypt, 1871.
Libretto by Ghislanzoni.

In the time of the Pharaohs, Egypt and Ethiopia are at war. Aïda, an Ethiopian slave girl, and Radames, Captain of the Egyptian guard, are secretly in love. Aïda's owner is the Pharaoh's daughter, Amneris, who expects to marry Radames. Aïda and Radames must choose between love for each other and love of their homeland.

Giuseppe Verdi
(1813–1901)

Guard the Nile
Sul del Nilo al sacro lido

Act I. Radames has been divinely chosen to lead the holy battle against Ethiopia. The King and court call on the Egyptians to defend the sacred Nile.

*An open-air production was given in 1912
at the foot of the pyramids of Egypt.*

Heavenly Aïda
Celeste Aïda

Act I. Radames sings the praise of Aïda as he leaves for his military mission.

Aïda at the Arena di Verona, Italy.

Glory to Egypt and Grand March
Gloria all'Egitto

Act III, Scene II. The King and his subjects receive the conquering army in a procession of soldiers, trumpeters, chariots, slaves, and dancing girls. This is one of the grandest scenes in all of opera.

10

The Return of Radames, Act II.

AMAHL AND THE NIGHT VISITORS

English
One act.
Premiered on NBC TV, December 24, 1951.
Libretto by Menotti.

The Three Wise Men are traveling from the east to Bethlehem to deliver their gifts at the manger of the Christ Child. They stop at the humble hut of a crippled child, Amahl, and his mother. Amahl asks the Magi to deliver his crutch as his own gift. When he presents it, he is miraculously cured and can walk again.

Gian-Carlo Menotti
(1911–2007)

Don't Cry, Mother Dear

Amahl's mother has been singing about their poverty and Amahl responds, trying to comfort her.

Don't Cry, Mother Dear

Don't cry Mother dear; don't worry for me.
If we must go begging, a good beggar I'll be.
I know sweet tunes to set people dancing.
We'll walk and walk from village to town—
  you dressed as a gypsy, and I as a clown.
At noon, we shall eat roast goose and sweet almonds.
At night we shall sleep with the sheep and the stars.
I'll play my pipes, you'll sing and you'll shout.
The windows will open and people lean out.
The king will ride by and hear your loud voice and
  throw us some gold to stop all the noise.
My dreamer, good night! You're wasting the light.
Good night!

THE BARBER OF SEVILLE

Il Barbiere di Siviglia
eel bahr-bea´-reh dee see-veel´-yah

Gioachino Rossini
(1794–1868)

Italian.
Two acts.
Premiered in Rome, 1816.
Libretto by Cesare Sterbini.

In eighteenth-century Spain, old Dr. Bartolo is the guardian of the young, lovely Rosina. He keeps her under lock and key, as he intends to marry her with the aid of her music teacher—an unscrupulous priest. Count Almaviva is a wealthy young nobleman who also desires to marry Rosina. Figaro, the local busybody barber, is ever resourceful in helping the Count gain entry to see Rosina. When Dr. Bartolo catches on, he finds a notary and hastens the man to his house to proceed with his own wedding plans. He stops to arrange for the police to come with him and arrest Figaro and the Count. The slight delay gives Rosina and the Count a few moments to trick the notary. Dr. Bartolo and the police arrive to find them lawfully and happily married.

Una voce poco fa
oon-a vō-chā pō-cō fä

A Small Voice I Hear

Act I, Scene II. Rosina is in Bartolo's house, holding a letter from the Count.

THE BARTERED BRIDE

Prodaná Nevěsta

Slovak/Czech
Three acts.
Premiered in Prague (then in Austria, now the Czech Republic), 1866.
Libretto by Savina.

Set in Bohemia in the 1800s. Maria's parents have chosen a husband for her—Wenzel, the son of Micha, a well-to-do villager. But Maria loves Hans, a poor farmhand, and will not agree. The marriage broker offers Hans a large sum of money to forego all claims on Maria. Hans pockets the money, signing a document "in favor of Micha's son." Maria is brokenhearted, but when all parties are together, Hans is recognized as Micha's long-lost elder son. Maria forgives Hans for "selling" her, and they are happily reunited.

Bedřich Smetana
(1824–1884)

Villager's Chorus
Seht am strauch die knaspen springen

Act I. Opening Chorus.

18

An open-air performance of The Bartered Bride *at Zoppsot,
near Danzig Gdansk, northern Poland/Germany.*

*The marriage broker is persuading Hans to forego all claims to Maria
by offering him three hundred gulden-cash,* Act II.

CARMEN

French.
Four acts.
Premiered in Paris, 1875.
Libretto by H. Meihac and L. Halevy.

In Spain, about 1820. Carmen, the beautiful gypsy girl, is sought by Don José, who deserts his regiment to live with her in a mountain retreat of gypsy smugglers. She loves him, but soon discards him for Escamillo, the most popular toreador (bullfighter) in Seville. A jealous rage results in her death by stabbing.

Georges Bizet
(1838–1875)

Toreador Song
Votre toast je peux vous le rendre

Act II. At a Spanish tavern, Escamillo arrives in a procession and sings this famous song.

A wild and rocky pass in the mountains, Act III.

The death of Carmen, Act IV.

CAVALLERIA RUSTICANA

kah-vahl-lay-ree´-ah roos-tih-kah´-nah

Rustic Chivalry

Italian.
One act.
Premiered in Rome, 1890.
Libretto by G. Targioni-Tozzetti and G. Menasci.

Church bells chime in a small Sicilian village as peasants are singing and celebrating Easter morning. Turiddu, a village youth, has returned from the war to find that Lola, his betrothed, has married someone else. He had also courted another village maiden who is expecting his child, but he rejects her and she is facing dishonor. Lola has a change of heart and meets him secretly. The rustic code of honor results in a duel.

Pietro Mascagni
(1863–1945)

Intermezzo

After an argument and scuffle amongst the four youths, the village square is now empty. The orchestra plays this Intermezzo.

22

23

Easter Hymn
Regina Coeli
(Fragment)

The church and village square on Easter morning, Act I.

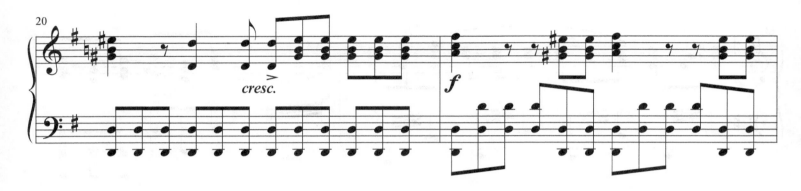

Lola is drawing Turiddu's affection away from Santuzza.

DER ROSENKAVALIER
der ro'zen kava'lir

The Knight of the Rose

German
Three acts.
Premiered in Dresden, Germany, 1911.
Libretto by Hofmannsthal.

Set in a palace in Vienna in the 1740s. While her husband is away, a middle-aged princess is pursuing the handsome young nobleman, Octavian. Her older country cousin, a Baron, arrives at the palace to plan his marriage to young Sophie, daughter of a local merchant. The Baron uses Octavian to present Sophie with a silver rose, which is the traditional love token. At the rose ceremony, Sophie and Octavian are immediately attracted to each other, and Sophie finds the Baron most undesirable. Through a series of tricks, the Baron is outmaneuvered in his love quest for Sophie, and the princess has to resign herself to losing Octavian to a girl of his own age.

Richard Strauss
(1864–1949)

Waltz

Act II. The Baron is attempting to show affection for Sophie.

27

Arrival of the Rosenkavalier, Act II.

DIE FLEDERMAUS
dēē flā´-der-maus

The Bat

German
Three acts.
Premiered in Vienna, Austria, 1874.
Libretto by Haffnert Genee after Meilhac, Halevy, and Benedix.

Set in Vienna in the 1800s. Dr. Falke attends a costume ball dressed as a bat. He drinks until he is a bit beyond tipsy, so his "friend" puts him out on a park bench for the night. He awakens the next morning to the laughter of passersby, and begins to make plans to get even. What follows is a comedy of manners involving the friend's wife and maid, a prince, a prison director, a musician, and a lawyer. In the end, they have a toast together, and agree that champagne is to blame for the events.

Johann Strauss, Jr.
(1825–1899)

Csárdás
chär-däsh

Gypsy Dance

Act II. Rosalinde attends a ball, disguising herself as a Hungarian countess in order to observe her husband. She enchants him with this dance.

29

30

Courtesy of the Metropolitan Archives.

Rosalinde finds her husband Eisenstein and Alfred in jail, Act III.

DIE MEISTERSINGER VON NÜRNBERG

dēē mis´-ter-sing-er von Nyrnberk

The Mastersingers of Nuremberg

German
Three acts.
Premiered in Munich, Germany, 1868.
Libretto by Wagner.

Richard Wagner
(1813–1883)

Set in Nuremberg, Germany, in the 1500s. The Mastersingers Guild has a picky list of rules for correct presentation of poetry and music. One of the members, a wealthy goldsmith, has promised his lovely daughter, Eva, in marriage to the next winner of the grand song contest. The town clerk wants Eva for himself, so using the guild rules, he manages to disqualify Sir Walter, a knight who is in love with Eva. Hans, a cobbler, concocts a scheme to help Sir Walter enter and win the contest, and Eva is able to bestow the wreath of victory upon him.

March of the Mastersingers

Act III, Scene II. The guilds march to the contest, some in boats. A charming river scene.

Eva bestows the Wreath of Victory, Act III.

DON GIOVANNI

don jo-vän'nē

Don Juan

Italian
Two acts.
Premiered in Prague, 1787.
Libretto by Lorenzo da Ponte.

Set in Seville, Spain, in the 1600s. Don Giovanni is a dashing Spanish nobleman with talents for sword fighting, romantic conquests, and fast escapes. He has cast aside Anna, then Elvira, and is attempting to attract Zerlina, a pretty peasant girl. His servant recites a catalog list of Giovanni's courtings—640 in Italy alone. He has many enemies lurking. In the pale moonlight of the cathedral square, he sees the statue of Anna's father, whom he killed in a duel. He jokingly invites it to a regal feast at his castle. The banquet is in full swing when a heavy tread is heard: the stone statue has arrived. It seizes Giovanni and carries him down into the hellfires.

Wolfgang Amadeus Mozart
(1756–1791)

Give Me Your Hand, Zerlina
Là ci darem la mano

Act I. At a wedding party, the Don detains Zerlina, the bride-to-be, and flatters her until she is impressed. They sing this duet.

Arranged by Sherron Adrian.

34

Zerlina is on the balcony, the Don below. He has changed clothes with his servant and is hiding his mandolin.
He pushes his servant forward to speak for him, Act II, Scene I.

The stone statue speaks to the Don and his companion. The inscription reads:
"The revenge awaits here my murderer," Act II, Scene II.

THE ELIXIR OF LOVE

L'Elisir D'Amore
lay-lee-zeer´ dam-oh´-reh

Italian
Two acts.
Premiered in Milan, Italy, 1832.
Libretto by Felice Romani, after Daniel Auber and Eugene Scribe.

Set in a small Italian village in the nineteenth century. Nemorino, a young peasant, is lovesick for Adina, a charming village maiden. She is planning to marry the sergeant of the village garrison. Nemorino is reluctant to press his case, as he is penniless. Dr. Dulcamara, a traveling quack, claims to be the inventor of a love potion that will change your desired one's indifference to burning passion. Around the same time, the peasant girls learn that Nemorino's uncle has died, and left him a handsome property. When Adina sees sixteen village girls shamelessly flirting with him, she becomes jealous and also wants him. The villagers now believe that the elixir brings love—and riches—and so the "doctor" is able to dispose of his entire supply and move on.

Gaetano Donizetti
(1797–1848)

Una furtiva lagrima
Down Her Cheek a Pearly Tear

Act II. Adina regrets being cool to Nemorino. He sees her crying and sings this famous air.

Courtesy of the Metropolitan Archives.

Dr. Dulcamara arrives to promote his elixir, Act I.

EUGENE ONEGIN

Yevgény Onégin

Russian
Three acts.
Premiered in Moscow, Russia, 1879.
Libretto by Tchaikovsky and Shidlovsky based on Pushkin's poem.

Set at a Russian estate near St. Petersburg in the 1820s. Two friends, the poet, Lenski, and Eugene Onegin, arrive at the country estate of two young sisters, Olga and Tatiana. Olga is Lenski's fiancée. Tatiana is attracted to the handsome, gallant Onegin, and sends him a long love letter. He coldly replies that she should restrain her emotions, as he would tire of married life to a country girl. He attends a ball and flirts with Olga, which enrages Lenski. A duel follows, and Onegin kills his friend. Later, when Onegin is weary of his empty life, he meets Tatiana at a ball. She is now a dazzling, begowned hostess, married to a prince. Onegin begs her to leave her husband for him, and although she still loves Onegin, out of honor Tatiana will not abandon her husband. Tchaikovsky left us this haunting love song.

Peter Ilyich Tchaikovsky
(1840–1893)

Tatiana Writes a Love Letter

The Berlin Opera's striking setting of the duel scene, Act II, Scene II.

FAUST
fowst

French.
Five acts.
Premiered in Paris, 1859.
Libretto by Barbier and Carre, based on Goethe's tragedy.

Set in a German village in the sixteenth century. Faust, a lonely, embittered philosopher, promises his soul to the Devil in exchange for his lost youth and the beautiful young maiden, Marguerite.

Angel Hosts
Anges purs, anges radieux

Charles F. Gounod
(1818–1893)

Act V. Marguerite, in prison for destroying her child, is saved by a company of angels.

45

The aged Faust in his studio of musty scrolls and scientific supplies. He is planning to drink a poisonous draught,
Act I.

46

Marguerite longs for Faust's return, Act III.

Marguerite's brother and the soldiers return from the wars, Act IV.

GIANNI SCHICCHI

ji-an-ni skee-kee

Italian
One act.
Premiered in New York, 1918.
Libretto by G. Forzane

Set in Florence, Italy, in 1299. A wealthy mill owner, Donati, has died. In his bedchamber are relatives who are weeping, praying, and pretending to mourn while frantically searching for his will. When they find it, alas! Donati has left everything to the monastery. The relatives agree on a scheme. They hide the dead body and Gianni Schicchi gets into the sickbed in disguise, calling in a notary to record a new will.

Giacomo Puccini
(1858–1924)

O, mio babbino caro
Oh, My Beloved Daddy

Gianni Schicchi's daughter is begging him for permission to marry Donati's nephew. He agrees and, in the new will, also gives them the grand house.

The new will is drawn up.

Courtesy of the Metropolitan Archives.

HANSEL AND GRETEL

Hansel und Gretel

haen'-zel oondt gray'-tel

Engelbert Humperdinck
(1854–1921)

German
Three acts.
Premiered in Weimar, Germany, 1893.
Libretto by Adeleid Wette, after Grimm.

Hansel and Gretel live happily with their parents in a tumble-down hut in the woods. When the children become lost while picking berries, they spend the night under a tree while fourteen angels watch over them. When morning comes, they are lured to a cozy gingerbread house, the home of a wicked witch who seizes them.

Evening Prayer

Act II, Scene II. In a dream scene, angels are hovering over the sleeping children.

52

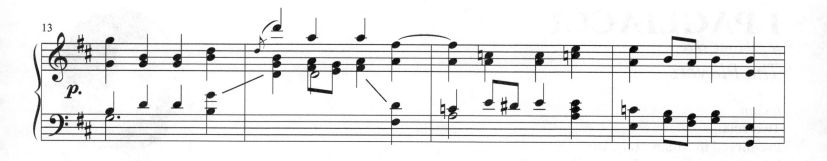

Hansel and Gretel meet the old witch, Act III.

When at night I go to sleep,
Fourteen angels watch do keep:

Two my head protecting,
Two my feet directing,

Two do guard me on the right,
Two upon my left in sight,

Two there are who warmly cover,
Two above me always hover,

Two to whom the word is given
To guide my steps to heaven.

I PAGLIACCI
ee pahl-yat'-chee

The Players

Italian
Two acts.
Premiered in Milan, Italy, 1892.
Libretto by Leoncavallo.

Set in a small Italian village in the 1860s. A caravan of entertainers arrives and erects a portable theater. By coincidence, the evening's play is quite like a drama going on among the actors, involving a faithless wife, an outraged husband, the wounded pride of another suitor, and a wealthy local farmer pursuing the same actress. This would-be comedy ends in violence.

Ruggiero Leoncavallo
(1858–1919)

Canio, the outraged husband, stabs his wife's secret lover, while screaming "la commedia è finita" (the comedy has ended), Act II.

E vo-i
I Pray You
(Cantabile from the Prologue)

Prologue. Tonio, dressed as a clown, speaks to the audience about the plot, and then orders the curtain to rise.

Vesti la giubba

ves-tēē lä jēē-ub-bä

On With the Play

This song is sung with great pathos, including a directive to let the voice crack at measure 26.
Caruso's recording in 1904 was the first classical music record to sell a million copies.

Act I. Canio almost stabs his wife but is restrained by Peppe. He now sits alone in shame and regret.

Arrival of the players, Act I.

Queen Elizabeth II of England arrives at the Paris Opera, France, April 8, 1957. British photographer Bert Hardy.

I PURITANI

ee poo-ree-tah'-nee

The Puritans

Italian
Three acts.
Premiered in Paris, France, 1835.
Libretto by Carlo Peopli, after Ancelot and Saintine, after Scott's "Old Mortality."

Set in Plymouth, England, in 1635, shortly after the execution of Charles I during the English Crown's war with the Puritans. Elvira, the Puritan governor's daughter, loves Lord Arthur, a royalist. Her father consents to their marriage. Arthur discovers that the late King's widow is a prisoner in the castle, and he helps her escape by disguising her in Elvira's wedding veil. Elvira learns that Arthur was seen deserting her with a veiled woman, and she becomes mentally unbalanced. When Arthur returns for her, he is arrested. A Puritan victory is announced, including amnesty for all prisoners. Elvira regains her reason and is united with Arthur.

Vincenzo Bellini
(1801–1835)

Sound the Trumpet
Suoni la tromba

Act II. After Lord Arthur is pardoned, Sir George and Sir Richard, the Puritans, sing this duet, pledging to fight together for their country.

IL TROVATORE
il trō-vä-tō'rā

The Troubadour

Italian
Four acts.
Premiered in Rome, 1853.
Libretto by Cammarano, after Guitierrez.

Set in fifteenth-century Spain. The troubadour Manrico is leader of the rebel army. Count di Luna is leading the king's army. Leonora is the maiden that they both wish to marry, and Manrico has been serenading her. Di Luna's men arrest an old gypsy woman because they believe she caused the death of di Luna's infant brother many years ago. Manrico tries to rescue her, as it is rumored that she may be his true mother, but he is caught and imprisoned. To secure Manrico's freedom, Leonora offers herself to di Luna, then takes poison. Feeling tricked, di Luna has Manrico executed. The gypsy woman then reveals to di Luna that it was her own child that died years ago, and that di Luna has just killed his own "missing" brother.

Giuseppe Verdi
(1813–1901)

Home to Our Mountains
Ai nostri monti

Act IV, Scene II. Manrico and the gypsy Azucena are in prison. They sing of happier days in the past.

60

The ramparts of Aliaferia, Act IV.

The convent near Castellor, Act II.

LA BOHÈME

lah boh-ehm'

Bohemian Life

Italian. Four acts.
Premiered in Turin, Italy, 1896.
Libretto by G. Giacosa and L. Illica.

Set in the Latin Quarter of Paris, about 1830. Four artistic friends share a cold garret.
Though confident of a dazzling future, it is Christmas Eve, and they are without fuel
and food. Then one of them arrives with money, wine, and supplies. They go out to
celebrate, leaving Rudolfo, the poet, to finish an article. Mimi, a frail girl who lives in
a room above, knocks at his door, needing a light for her candle.

Giacomo Puccini
(1858–1924)

Musetta's Waltz
Quando me'n vo

Act II. At a student café, Marcel's old flame, Musetta, arrives and wishes to reconcile.

63

A cold and cheerless dawn in the city, Act II.

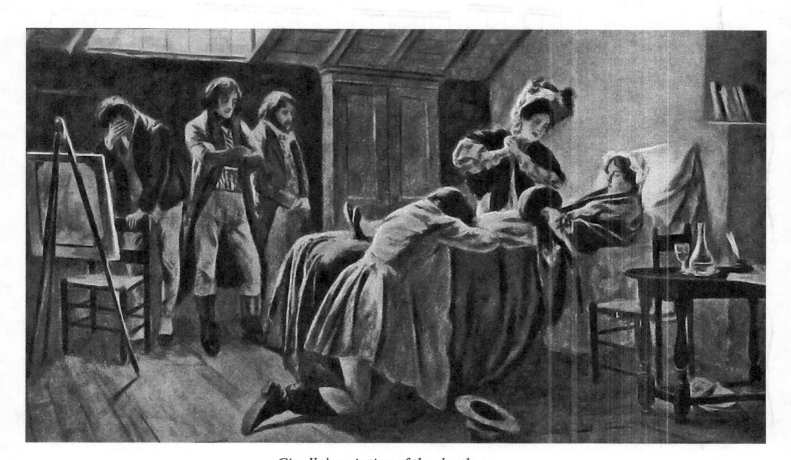

Cipolla's painting of the death scene.

L'AFRICAINE
laf-ree-kahn
The African Maiden

Italian (French title)
Five acts.
Premiered in Paris, France, 1865.
Libretto by Eugene Scribe.

Vasco da Gama, the Portuguese explorer, returns with two African prisoners. The plot takes many turns, ending with the African woman Selika's suicide under a poisonous manchineel tree in India. A long opera, which can take two evenings without cuts, it is performed only rarely today. But this tenor solo lives on.

Giacomo Meyerbeer
(1791–1864)

O Paradiso
Oh Paradise
Excerpt

Act IV. The Indian priests condemn Vasco to die. As he looks out on this beautiful land of his dreams, he sings "Oh, Paradise."

Andantino

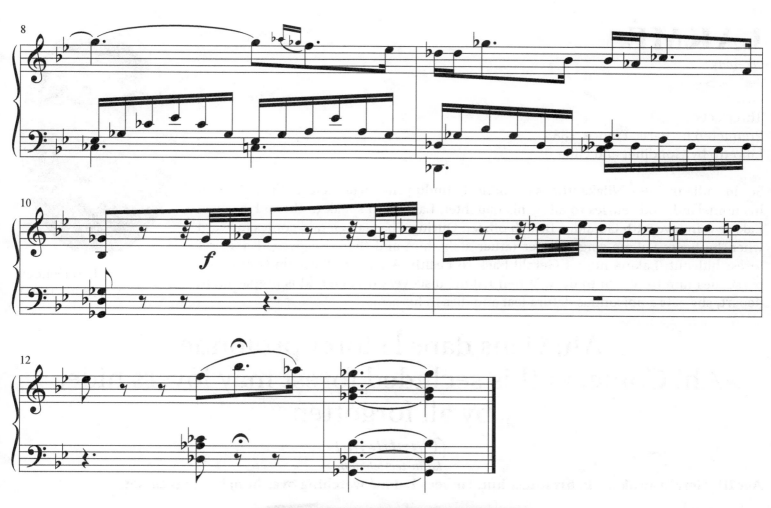

Enrico Caruso as Vasco da Gama.

LAKMÉ
lák'-may'

French
Three acts.
Premiered in Paris, France, 1883.
Libretto by Gondinet and Gilie.

Leo Delibes
(1836–1891)

Set in India in 1880. Nilakantha is a fanatical Hindu priest who detests the British in his homeland, and refuses to allow his daughter, Lakmé, to speak to them. However, Lakmé is in love with Gerald, a British officer. During a bazaar, Gerald comes forward when he hears Lakmé singing. Her father stabs him and then escapes. At a secret forest hideout, Lakmé nurses Gerald back to health. A fellow officer finds him and persuades him to return to duty. When Lakmé discovers that Gerald is preparing to depart, she eats a poisonous datura leaf and dies in his arms.

Ah, viens dans la forêt profonde
Ah! Come, in this secluded forest may lovers hide, by all forgotten

(Cantilene)
kahn-tee-leh'noh

Act III. Gerald awakens in his forest hut. He sees Lakmé watching over him; he sings to her.

68

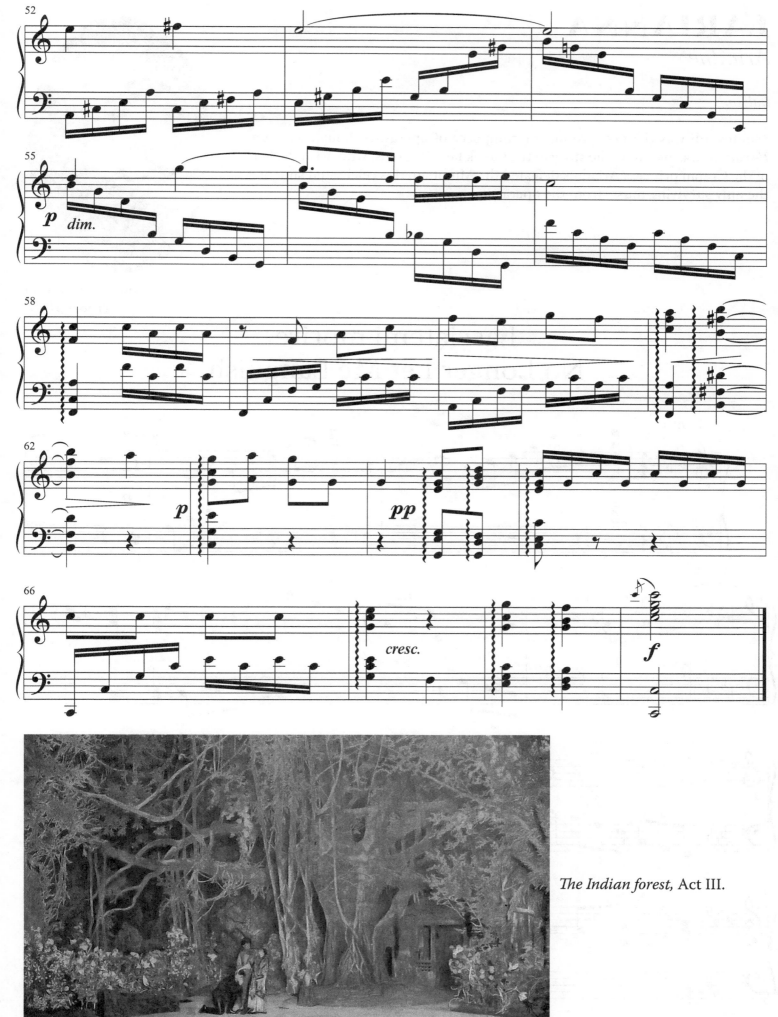

The Indian forest, Act III.

L'ARIANNA
Ariadne

Italian.

Monteverdi was the first prominent composer of operas. Although we know *L'Arianna* was based on the story of the Greek hero Theseus, who, with the help of the Cretan princess Ariadne, defeated the Minotaur, this celebrated lament is the only surviving music from the opera.

Claudio Monteverdi
(1567–1643)

Lasciatemi morire
No Longer Let Me Languish

72

LA TRAVIATA

lah trah-vee-ah'-tah

The Strayed Woman

Italian
Three acts.
Premiered in Venice, Italy, 1853
Libretto by Piave, based on Dumas.

Alfredo, a young nobleman, loves the beautiful though ill courtesan, Violetta. They retire to a happy country life near Paris. Soon Alfredo's father arrives and begs Violetta to give up his son, as the scandal threatens Alfredo's sister's chances for a respectable marriage. Violetta reluctantly agrees and goes to Paris. Alfredo finds her there in the company of a former admirer and a duel follows. When Alfredo learns of Violetta's sacrifice for him, he rushes to her sickbed. But her health is waning, and she dies just as they are reunited.

Giuseppe Verdi
(1813–1901)

Drinking Song

Act I. At a party, Violetta and Alfredo become attracted to each other. Together they lead this rousing song.

Courtesy of the Metropolitan Archives.

Alfredo's father visits Violetta. He asks her to leave Alfredo and return to Paris, Act II.

Amami, Alfredo
My Beloved Alfredo

Act II, Scene I. After Alfredo's father makes his visit to Violetta, she sings this farewell love song.

LE PROPHÈTE

le prō-fāt'

The Prophet

French
Five acts.
Premiered in Paris, France, 1849.
Libretto by Scribe.

Set in Holland in 1536. A youth named John wishes to marry Bertha, a beautiful peasant girl. In order to marry, Bertha must have the consent of the Count, her overlord, but he wants Bertha for himself. The Count imprisons Bertha and John's mother. John leads a successful peasant revolt and is to be crowned Prophet-King, but a series of tragic events follows.

Giacomo Meyerbeer
(1791–1864)

Coronation March

Act IV. John is marching into Munster Cathedral.

Arranged by the composer.

John denying his mother, Act IV.

LOHENGRIN

loh'-en-grin

German
Three acts.
Premiered in Weimar, Germany, 1850.
Libretto by Wagner.

In this medieval legend, Lohengrin is a knight of the Holy Grail. If his identity is revealed, he must return to the brotherhood. A vow of secrecy is exacted from his beloved Elsa, but she breaks it, prompted by jealous advisers. This *Bridal Chorus* and Mendelssohn's *Wedding March* were linked together at the 1858 wedding of Princess Victoria of England and Prince Frederick William of Prussia, and thus began a music tradition of one hundred-plus years. Wagner's publisher accepted the rights to Lohengrin in 1851 as payment of a debt for a concert grand piano.

Richard Wagner
(1813–1883)

Faithful and True
Treulich gefürt
(Bridal Chorus)

Act III. The great doors of the bridal chamber open as Elsa and Lohengrin enter, accompanied by ladies and nobles.

Arranged by the composer.

The arrival of Lohengrin, Act I.

LUCIA DI LAMMERMOOR

loo-chee'ah dee lah-mair-moor

Lucy of Lammermoor

Italian

Three acts.
Premiered in Naples, Italy, 1835.
Libretto by S. Cammarano, after Sir Walter Scott's novel.

Gaetano Donizetti
(1797–1848)

War, revolution, and clan infighting have depleted the vast estates of the Scottish barons. The families of both Lucy and Edgar desperately need money and political connections. But they are in love and secretly exchange vows and rings before Edgar leaves on a mission to France. Lucy's brother stakes his future on marrying her to a wealthy Lord. He withholds Edgar's love letters from France and forges a letter implying that Edgar has been unfaithful. Under duress, Lucy agrees to marry Lord Bucklaw. Edgar arrives at the celebration and denounces Lucy and her family. That night, she is seized with madness and stabs her new husband, then dies herself by morning. Bells are tolling as Edgar hears of it. In grief and remorse, he stabs himself, praying to be united with his bride in heaven.

Esci, fuggi, il furor

es-shēē, fu-jēē

Leave Us

Act II. Edgar asks Lucy if she signed a marriage contract with Lord Bucklaw. He goes into a rage and tears it up.

Lucia, on her knees, praying

*The great hall of the
castle, Act II, Scene II.*

85

Prelude for Harp
Adapted

Act I, Scene II. Lucy, beside a moonlit fountain, is waiting for a tryst with Edgar.

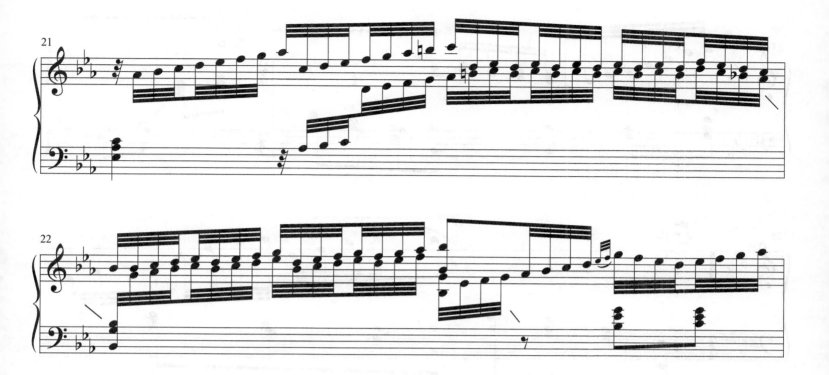

The Bride of Lammermoor, by Millais.

MADAMA BUTTERFLY
Madame Butterfly

Italian
Two acts.
Premiered in Milan, Italy, 1904.
Libretto by Illica and Giacosa (play by Belasco, story by J. L. Long).

Lieutenant Pinkerton, an American naval officer, is marrying a young Japanese geisha maiden. However, he intends to stay married only while his fleet is at Nagasaki. Butterfly devotes herself to his happiness, even renouncing her religion for his. Her family deserts her. Lt. Pinkerton soon leaves. He returns three years later with an American wife. Butterfly has borne him a son and has waited patiently for his promised return to her. When she realizes that he wants only his child, she stabs herself and dies, as Pinkerton expresses remorse for his actions.

Giacomo Puccini
(1858–1924)

Humming Chorus

Act II. Lt. Pinkerton has returned and his ship is in the harbor. Butterfly and her child are keeping vigil through the moonlit night.

The marriage ceremony, Act I.

THE MAGIC FLUTE

Die Zauberflöte

dee tsow-ber-floh'-ten

German

Two acts.

Premiered in Vienna, Austria, 1791, with Mozart himself conducting.

Libretto by Schikaneder and Giesecke, after Wieland.

Legendary Egypt. The story line is absurd and full of fantasy, giving Tamino's flute a magical power to control birds, reptiles, men, and the weather. Prince Tamino attempts to rescue the Queen of the Night's daughter, Pamina, from an evil sorcerer. Papageno, the Queen's birdcatcher, goes with him. The Queen gives them a magic flute and a glockenspiel for protection. They become separated and endure many trials, but both are rewarded with a mate. The sorcerer proclaims a victory of light over the powers of darkness.

Wolfgang Amadeus Mozart
(1756–1791)

O Isis und Osiris

Act II. In the temple of Wisdom, the priests bless the lovers, Tamino and Pamina.

94

The great invocation scene, Act II.

Papageno's Silver Bells

Act II. Papageno, the bird catcher, uses his magic bells to find his way to a pretty wife and a good dinner.

MANON

man'-on

French
Five acts.
Premiered in Paris, France, 1884.
Libretto by Meilhac and Gille after Prevost's *Manon Lescaut*.

Set in France, 1721. Manon is a country school girl on her way to a convent against her wishes. En route, she meets a young cavalier, des Grieux (*day cree-uh*), who is destined for the priesthood. They elope to Paris, but des Grieux's father has him abducted and brought home. Meanwhile, Manon has attracted the attention of a rich nobleman. After awhile, she tires of the life of luxury. She hears that the despondent des Grieux is about to enter a monastery, she rushes to him and they reunite. But des Grieux has to gamble to support Manon in the style she demands. He is falsely accused of cheating and is arrested, but then freed by the intervention of his father. Manon is then arrested as a dissolute woman. Des Grieux comes to her rescue just as soldiers are taking her to a prison colony. She asks des Grieux for forgiveness for her excesses, but is exhausted and dies in his arms.

Jules Massenet
(1842–1912)

Let Be No Sorrowing and Sighing
Profitons bien de la jeunesse

(Gavotte)

găh-vŏht'

Act III. On a street in Paris, Manon sings a happy tune for friends.

97

On the Havre Road, Manon asks for and receives forgiveness from Des Grieux, and then dies in his arms, Act V.

THE MARRIAGE OF FIGARO

Le Nozze di Figaro
le not'-zeh dee fee'-gahr-oh

Italian
Four acts.
Premiered in Vienna, Austria, 1786.
Libretto by Lorenzo da Ponte, after Beaumarchais. Actually a sequel to Rossini's *The Barber of Seville,* although the Rossini opera came thirty years later.

Wolfgang Amadeus Mozart
(1756–1791)

Seventeenth-century Spain. Two of Count Almaviva's servants wish to marry: Figaro, his valet, and Susanna, a maid to the Countess. As the Count finds Susanna to be very attractive, he claims the feudal custom of *droit de seigneur* (*dwä dū sen-yor*), meaning "rights of the Lord." These rights covered farming, hunting, taxation, and spending the wedding night with the peasant girls in his employ. Figaro has his own impediment to the marriage, as he owes money to the elderly Marcellina. Her lawyer demands that Figaro marry Marcellina to settle the debt. With help from all concerned, and amid many comic scenes, Figaro and Susanna surmount the problems of their wedding day and the Count learns a lesson.

Silently Bending, Night's Shadows Fall
Voi che sapete
voy-kā-säpātā

Act II. Cheribino, the Countess's page, strums his guitar and sings of the delights and misery of love, "What is this feeling?".

The marriage of Susanna and Figaro, Act IV.

D.C. al fine

MARTHA

German
Four acts.
Premiered in Vienna, Austria, 1847.
Libretto by Friedrich W. Riese, after St. George's ballet.

Set in England, in 1710. Lady Henrietta is bored with the splendors of court life. She hears the local peasants singing on their way to the fair and wishes to go along. She and her faithful maid dress as peasants out for hire, and her chaperone, Tristan, reluctantly dresses as a farmer. At the fair, the girls meet two young farmers who are attracted by their charms. Under the false names of Martha and Julia, the girls, in jest, contract to be servants for one year. They are hastily packed off to the farm and put to menial work. Tristan arrives at night with a coach and helps the girls escape through a window. However, "Martha" has become attracted to one of the farmers, who is of unknown parentage. He is later found to be the lost son and heir of Lord Derby, making him suitable to marry "Martha." She gladly becomes his bride.

Friedrich von Flotow
(1812–1883)

How So Fair
Mi appari tutt'amor

Act III. Alone in a forest, the farmer Lionel sings of his hopeless passion for Martha.

The Fair Scene, Act I.

NABUCCO

na-boo'koh

(Shortened form of Nebuchadnezzar, King of Babylon, 605–562 BCE)

Italian
Four acts.
Premiered in Milan, Italy, 1842.
Libretto by Solera.

The story is set among the Israelites, who are exiled in Babylon (modern-day Iran) in 586 BCE. Just as they are about to be executed, Nabucco prays to their god, Jehovah, for forgiveness. The golden idol of Baal breaks into pieces as Nabucco proclaims his faith in Jehovah and sets the captives free. The grand chorus paraphrases Psalm 137 from the Hebrew scriptures: "How shall we sing the Lord's song in a strange land?"

Giuseppe Verdi
(1813–1901)

Va pensiero
Go, My Thoughts, on Gilded Wings
(Chorus of the Hebrew Slaves)

PRINCE IGOR
Knyaz Igor

Russian
Prologue and four acts.
Premiered in St. Petersburg, Russia, 1890.
Libretto by Borodin and Vladimir Stassoff, after an old chronicle by a twelfth-century monk. Music completed by Rimsky-Korsakov and Glazounov.

Set in a Russian town and Tartar camp in the year 1185. Prince Igor must lead his army against the Tartar tribe, that has invaded southern Russia. He appoints his unreliable brother-in-law as Regent during his absence. He leaves his beloved wife, Princess Yaroslavna, but his son goes with him. Their army suffers defeat, and Prince and son are held prisoner at the Tartar camp. The son is enchanted by the Tartar ruler's daughter, and they decide to marry. News reaches the camp that Prince Igor's town has been sacked. In despair, Igor seeks an avenue of escape. His guard, who is a Christian convert, offers him a horse. As he enters his home town, there is great rejoicing, and he is united with the Princess.

Alexander Borodin
(1833–1887)

Polovetsian Dance
First Theme

Act II. As Prince Igor is an honored captive, he is entertained by the slave dancers of the Khan.

Arranged by Sherron Adrian

Prince Igor departs for the war, Act I.

RIGOLETTO
ri-gō-let'tō

Italian
Three acts.
Premiered in Venice, Italy, 1851.
Libretto by Piave, based on Victor Hugo's *Le roi s'amuse.*

Set in Italy, in the 1500s. At the brilliant court of a Duke lives Rigoletto, an embittered court jester. He bemoans his profession as a procurer of young maidens for the Duke. His sole joy in life is his daughter, Gilda, who he protects by keeping her hidden. Rigoletto's endless scheming has made him many court enemies. One of the Counts sees him visiting Gilda's cottage nightly and assumes she is his mistress. The Count abducts her and delivers her to the Duke. In revenge, Rigoletto hires an assassin and lures the Duke to a lonely inn. The assassin's sister is in sympathy with the Duke and convinces her brother to kill the next patron instead. Gilda enters next. She is murdered and her body delivered in a sack to Rigoletto. He drags it to the river and, upon opening the sack, finds Gilda dying. He falls senseless on her body.

Giuseppe Verdi
(1813–1901)

Dearest Name
Caro nome

Act I, Scene II. Gilda is charmed by the Duke, disguised as a student. After he departs, she sings to herself.

Frieda Hempel, German opera singer, as Gilda.

RINALDO
ree-nhal'-doh

Italian
Three acts.
Premiered in London, England, 1711.
Libretto by Adam Hill.

Rinaldo is a Knight Templar involved in the love triangle of his military commander. The opera was mounted with great splendor and realism, including live birds in the magic garden. This beautiful air lingers in the heart of everyone who hears it.

George Frideric Handel
(1685–1759)

Lascia ch'io pianga
läsh'-shä kē-ō pēē-än'-gäh
Let Me Cry

Act I. Almirena, daughter of a noble, laments her capture by a sorceress.

115

SAMSON ET DALILA

sam-sohn ay dah-lee-lah

Samson and Delilah

French
Three acts.
Premiered in Weimar, Germany, 1877.
Libretto by Ferdinand Lemaire, from the Old Testament book of Judges.

In 1150 BCE, the Israelites are enslaved by the Philistines. Samson, an Israeli, kills a Philistine leader and incites a successful revolt. However, the Philistine High Priest has a beautiful and wily daughter, Delilah, who seduces Samson and then betrays him by cutting off his hair, the source of his strength. Shorn, blind, and imprisoned, he prays for a return of his great strength. During a celebration, a small boy leads him to the marble pillars which support the Philistine temple. Samson overturns them, crushing all as the temple crumbles.

Camille Saint-Saëns
(1835–1921)

My Heart at Thy Sweet Voice
Mon coeur s'ouvre á ta voix

Act II. Delilah sings of love and passion for Samson, then asks him to confide the secret plans of the Hebrews.

Samson, blind and head bowed in prayer, is led by a page to the great pillars of the temple, Act III, Scene II.

117

Dance of the Philistine maidens, Act III, Scene II.

TALES OF HOFFMANN

Les Contes D'Hoffmann
le kongt doff'mahn

French
Three acts.
Premiered in Paris, France, 1881.
Libretto by Jules Barbier. Music completed by Guiraud in 1881.

Set in Germany in the 1800s. A group of students are enjoying an evening at a beer cellar in Nuremberg. Hoffmann tells them three stories of his unfortunate love interests: Olympia, a mechanical doll, Lady Giulietta, a Viennese beauty, and Antonio, who dies from too much singing. The students urge Hoffmann to forget the past and the Muse of Art comes to console him.

Jacques Offenbach
(1819–1880)

Barcarolle: Belle nuit, nuit d'amor
Boat Song: Lovely Night, Night of Love

Act II. Sung as a duet while Hoffmann is courting a Venetian lady.

119

120

121

TANNHÄUSER
tahn'-hoy-zer

German
Three acts.
Premiered in Dresden, Germany, 1845.
Libretto by Wagner.

Tannhäuser, a Minstrel-Knight, desires the hand of the lovely princess Elizabeth, but his emotions waver back to a year of erotic love spent with the evil enchantress, Venus. He presents himself in the Hall of Song to sing in a tournament, but when he takes up his harp, he sings the praise of Venus. He is ordered to travel with pilgrims to seek forgiveness from the Pope. When the pilgrims return, Tannhäuser is not with them. In Rome he was told that forgiveness for him is as impossible as the papal wooden staff sprouting leaves. The princess is heartbroken, and collapses and dies. The exhausted Tannhäuser returns in time to kneel at her bier, where he dies as well. Just then, pilgrims bring miraculous news that the papal staff in Rome has put forth green leaves and spring blossoms—the gates of heaven have opened for this troubled soul.

Richard Wagner
(1813–1883)

Pilgrim's Chorus
Beglückt darf nun dich

Act III, Scene I. The pilgrims are heard returning from Rome.

The Hall of Song, Act II.

Setting of Act III at the Metropolitan.

THAÏS
tah-ees'

French
Three acts.
Premiered in Paris, France, 1894.
Libretto by Gallet, after A. France.

Set in Alexandria, Egypt, early Christian era, 4th century. The monk Athanael feels he must convert the beautiful courtesan Thaïs from her life of physical pleasure. His friend Nicias, who has paid for a week of her love, introduces Thaïs to Athanael. He succeeds in converting her, and she agrees to enter a convent. Back at his own monastery, Athanael discovers that he has fallen in love with Thaïs. He goes to tell her of this only to find her dying, serene in her faith. He has saved a soul, but his improper intentions have compromised his own holy vow.

Jules Massenet
(1842–1912)

Meditation

Act II, Scene II. The orchestra presents this Meditation with the curtain down, symbolizing Thaïs' spiritual conversation. It is heard again as she is dying in Act II, Scene III.

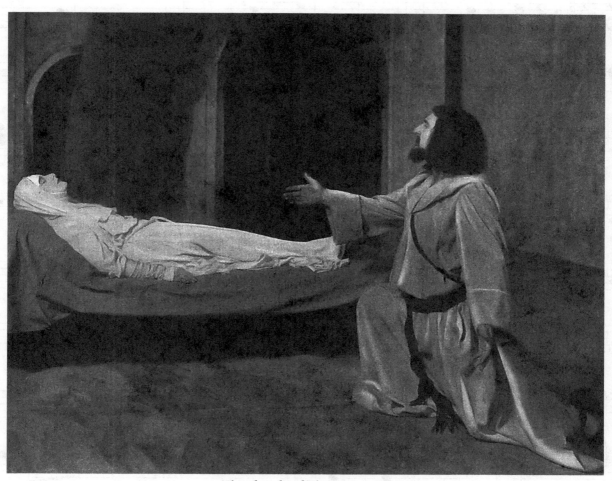

The death of Thaïs, Act II.

TOSCA
toss'-kah

Italian.

Three acts.

Premiered in Rome, Italy, 1900.

Libretto by Giuseppe Giacosa and Luigi Illica, after Sardou's *La Tosca*.

Set in Rome, in 1800. Tosca is a celebrated singer and vivacious beauty. She is to marry Mario, a painter of church murals. His childhood friend is now an escaped political prisoner, who finds Mario in the chapel. Mario helps to hide him. The brutal chief of police wants to marry Tosca, so he arrests Mario as an accomplice and sentences him to be tortured and shot. In desperation, Tosca begs the police chief for Mario's freedom—the price is her honor and revealing the hiding place of Mario's friend. The police chief also claims that Tosca must agree to a mock execution for the sake of appearances. When he tries to force his embrace on Tosca, she draws a knife from the table and stabs him in the heart. At the execution, real bullets are used, and Mario dies. Then soldiers come running in, announcing the murder of the police chief. Before they can arrest her, Tosca dashes to the castle parapet and leaps to her death.

Giacomo Puccini
(1858–1924)

I Lived for Art
Vissi d'Arte

Act II. Police Chief Scarpia has broken Tosca's will, claiming Mario will die. Weeping, she sings this sad air.

Tosca and Mario in the church, Act I.

The murder of Scarpia, Act II.

The death of Mario, Act II.

Palais Garnier, Paris, France.

TRISTAN UND ISOLDE

tris'-tahn oondt ees-zol'-deh

Tristan and Isolde

German
Three acts.
Premiered in Munich, Germany, 1865.
Libretto by Wagner.

Richard Wagner
(1813–1883)

Set in ancient times, near Cornwall, England, at sea. Princess Isolde of Ireland is sailing to England to become the bride of elderly King Mark. She accepts this loveless marriage as her duty, because it will bring peace between the two countries. Her escort, sent by the king, is his trusted nephew, Tristan. But Tristan and Isolde have fallen in love. Out of honor, Tristan feels he must avoid Isolde. She is so hurt by his coolness that she plans a parting drink of poison for both of them. Her maid stirs up a love potion instead, and the couple are soon embracing. Isolde marries the king, but she and Tristan spend secret hours together. A treacherous knight betrays them, and he and Tristan draw swords. Tristan is wounded and carried to his own distant castle. As Isolde arrives to tend his wound, he falls lifeless in her arms. She sinks in death beside him. King Mark arrives, intending to forgive and unite the two lovers, but it is too late.

Isolde's Love-Death

Act II, Scene III. When Isolde learns that Tristan is dead, her grief brings on this sad and sweet song. She dies at its end.

Tristan and Isolde confront each other aboard ship, Act I.

While King Mark is away with a hunting party, Isolde uses a torch
to signal for Tristan to come to her, Act II.

TURANDOT
ta-rahn'dō

Italian. Three acts.
Premiered in Milan, Italy, 1926.
Libretto by G. Adami and R. Simoni, after Schiller and Gozzi.

Set in Peking, China, in legendary times. The Emperor's courtiers—Ping, Pang, and Pong—lament that China was tranquil for 7,000 centuries until the birth of the cruel princess, Turandot. She has offered to marry the suitor who can solve three enigmas, but failure results in death. Thirteen have failed, and a fourteenth unknown prince now presents himself. Through courage, love, and matching wits, he is able to transform Turandot, who tearfully accepts him and begins a new and holy dawn for herself and country.

Giacomo Puccini
(1858–1924)

Nessun dorma
Let No One Sleep

Act III. The princess declares that no one shall sleep until the name of the prince is revealed.

Courtesy of the Metropolitan Archives.

The great square prepared for the contest of suitors, Act II.

Resources

Adler, Kurt. *Operatic Anthology, Volume V.* G. Schirmer. New York, 1904.

Anderson, James. *Harper Dictionary of Opera and Operetta.* Harper Collins. New York, 1989.

Apel, Wili. *Harvard Dictionary of Music,* 2nd. ed. Belknap/Harvard.

Baltzell, W. J. *Baltzell's Dictionary of Musicians.* Oliver Ditson Co. New York, 1911.

Bateman, Charles. *Piano Themes from Grand Opera.* Creative Concepts Publishing. Ojai, CA, 1993.

Bellini, Vincenzo. *I Puritani.* Score. Ricordi BMG. Italy, 2006.

Berger, William. *Wagner without Fear.* Vintage/Random House, Inc. New York, 1998.

Black Dog and Leventhal Publishers, NY.
  Aïda, CD Opera, Text, David Foil, 1966.
  Carmen, CD Opera, Text, David Foil, 1996.
  La Boheme, CD Opera, Text, David Foil, 1996.
  La Traviata, CD Opera, Text, Daniel S. Brink, 1998.
  Madame Butterfly, CD Opera, Text, Daniel S. Brink, 1998.
  Marriage of Figaro, CD Opera, Text, Robert Levine, 1996.

Blum, Daniel. *The Pictorial Treasury of Opera in America.* Grosset and Dunlap, Inc. New York, 1960.

Callinan, Comp. *School Songs.* Allyn and Bacon, 1938.

Camner, James, ed. *Great Composers in Historic Photographs.* Dover Publications. Mineola, NY, 1981.

Classical Fake Book, The. Hal Leonard Corp. Milwaukee, WI, 1992.

Cross, Donzella. *Music Stories for Boys and Girls.* Ginn & Co. Boston, 1926.

Cross, Milton and Karl Kohrs. *The New Complete Stories of Grand Opera.* Doubleday & Co. Garden City, NY, 1947.

Delibes, Leo. *Lakmé.* Vocal score. International Music Co. New York, 1973.

Donizetti, Gaetano. *Lucia di Lammermoor.* Opera score. G. Schirmer. New York, 1898.

England, Paul. *Fifty Favorite Operas.* Bonanza Books. New York, 1985.

Englemann, H. *Standard Opera Album.* Theodore Presser. Philadelphia, 1912.

Ewen, David. *The New Encyclopedia of the Opera.* Hill & Wang. New York, 1971.

France, Anatole. *Thaïs.* Illustrated Editions Co. New York, 1931.

Grabbee, P. and Nordoff. *Minute Stories of the Opera.* Grosset & Dunlap, Inc. New York, 1932.

Hall, Pauline. *Piano Time Opera.* Oxford University Press. London, 1998.

Hamilton, David. *The Metropolitan Opera Encyclopedia.* Simon and Schuster. New York, 1987.

Handel, G. F. *Rinaldo.* Vocal score. Barenreiter Kassel. London, 1998.

Howard, J. T. *The World's Great Operas.* Random House, Inc. New York, 1948.

Hughes, Spike. *Mozart's Great Operas.* Dover Publications. Mineola, NY, 1958.

International Library of Music, The, Volume 4. The University Society. New York, 1948.

Jacobs, A. and S. Sadie. *The Wordsworth Book of Opera.* Wordsworth Edition Ltd. England, 1996.

Lampe, J. B. *Star Songs from Grand Opera.* Jerome H. Remick & Co. New York, 1910.

Lampe, J. Bodewalt. *Piano Selections from the Opera.* Remick Music Corp. New York, 1911.

Larsen, R. L. and R. Walters, eds. *Mozart Arias.* Hal Leonard Corp. Milwaukee, WI, 1993.

Liszt, Franz. *Complete Piano Transcriptions from Wagner's Operas.* Dover Publications. Mineola, NY, 1981.

Liszt, Franz. *Piano Transcriptions from French and Italian Operas.* Charles Suttoni, comp. Dover Publications. Mineola, NY, 1982.

Massenet, Jules. *Manon.* Opera score. G. Schirmer. New York, 1963.

Menotti, Gian-Carlo. *Amahl and the Night Visitors.* Opera score. G. Schirmer. New York, 1997.

Morgenstern, Sam and Harold Barlow. *A Dictionary of Opera and Song Themes.* Crown Publishing, Inc. New York, 1950.

Mili, G. and M. E. Peltz. *The Magic of Opera.* Frederick A. Praeger, Inc. New York, 1960.

Neely, B. and R. Walters. *Opera at the Piano.* Hal Leonard Corp. Milwaukee, WI, 1998.

_____. *Opera's Greatest Melodies.* Hal Leonard Corp. Milwaukee, WI.

Preston, Stuart. *Farewell to the Old House.* Doubleday & Co. Garden City, NY, 1966.

Puccini for Easy Piano. Ricordi, 2002.

Puccini, Giacomo. "Nessun Dorma," from *Turandot.* Editions Henry Lemoine. Paris, 1997.

Puccini, Giacomo. "O Mio Babbine Caro," from *Gianni Schicchi.* Editions Henry Lemoine. Paris, 1999.

Rigoletto. Program notes. Wiener Staatsoper, 1994–95.

Rous, S. H. *The Victrola Book of the Opera,* 4th ed. Victor Talking Machine Co. Camden, NJ, 1917.

Rutter, John. *Opera Choruses.* Oxford University Press. London, 1995.

Simon, Henry W. *A Treasury of Grand Opera.* Simon and Schuster. New York, 1946.

Slater, Heather, compiler. Various arrangers. *Opera's Greatest Hits*. Amsco Publications. New York, 2007.

Stanley, Albert. *Favorite Opera Highlights*. Dover Publications. Mineola, NY, 2005.

Strauss, Jr., Johann. *Die Fledermaus*. Vocal score. Dover Publications. Mineola, NY, 2001.

Strauss, Richard. *Der Rosenkavalier*. Vocal score. Arr. Otto Singer. Dover Publications. Mineola, NY, 1987.

Tchaikovsky, Peter I. *Eugene Onegin*. Score. G. Schirmer, Inc. New York, 1957.

Various. *The World's Most Beloved Instrumental Music*. SongDex, Inc. New York, 1955.

Various authors. *The Decca Book of Opera*. Werner-Laurie. London, 1956.

Verdi, Giuseppe. *Il Trovatore*. Opera score. Ricordi.

Verdi, Giuseppe. *La Traviata*. Score. G. Schirmer, Inc. New York, 1946.

Wagner, Richard. *Tristan and Isolde*. Opera score. Dover Publications. Mineola, NY, 2003.

Wier, Albert E. *The Ideal Home Music Library, Volume V*. Charles Scribner's Sons. New York.

Acknowledgements

"Don't Cry, Mother Dear" from Amahl and the Night Visitors by Gian-Carlo Menotti. Copyright (c) 1951 (revised) by G. Schirmer, Inc. (ASCAP). International copyright secured. All rights reserved. Used by permission of the publisher.

Photo Credits

Cover, Teatro de San Carlo, Naples, Italy, built 1737, restoration completed 2010, photo Luciano Romano. Page 59, Queen Elizabeth at Paris Opera, photo by Bert Hardy, fifteen frames joined, Getty Images. *Victrola Book of Opera*, 4th ed., S. H. Rous, Victor Talking Machine Co., Camden, NJ 1917: pages 19, 21, 25, 26, 29, 31, 33, 35, 36, 41, 44, 46, 47, 48, 54, 56, 60, 61, 65, 67, 71, 80, 85, 86, 95, 102, 105, 112, 114, 118, 119, 124, 125, 128, 130, 135, 137. Pages 53, 82, *Music Stories for Boys and Girls*, Ginn & Co., 1926. Page 21, Carmen sketch, *A Treasury of Grand Opera*, cover, Simon & Schuster, NY, 1946. Page 100, engraving by Antonin-Marie Chatiemer, b. 1828. Page 36, title page from piano score by August Eberhard Muller of Mozart's *Don Giovanni*, published by S. A. Steiner of Vienna, 1810. Pages 13, 27, 98, *Great Composers*, Dover.